BOOK OF HAND DRAWN CROSSES

A Coloring Book For Teenagers and Adults

20 Unique Designs

By Artist, Ronnie Rosas

All Glory to God - Deuteronomy 32:2

Introduction

We hope you enjoy this coloring book of hand-drawn cross designs. Each design is unique and drawn freehand, with no rulers, grids, or other drawing instruments. All drawings were created with various pencils and/or pens. The drawings were developed through a series of stream-of-consciousness methods, mostly while sitting on the beach in Maui, South America, and Southern California. This first version is a picture book intended for use as a coloring book. We hope you enjoy the meditation of intricate coloring as much as Ronnie enjoyed hand-drawing each of his designs.

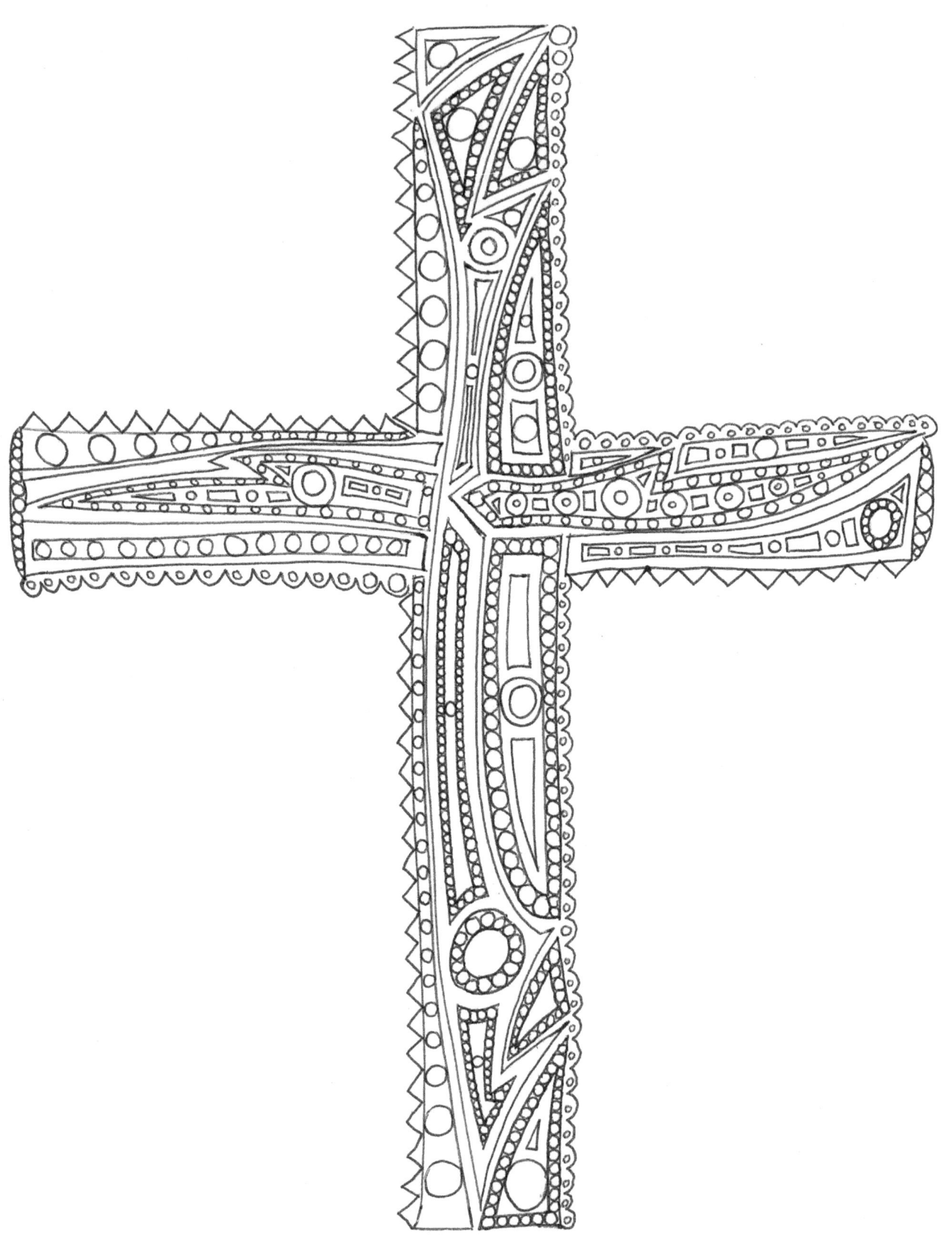

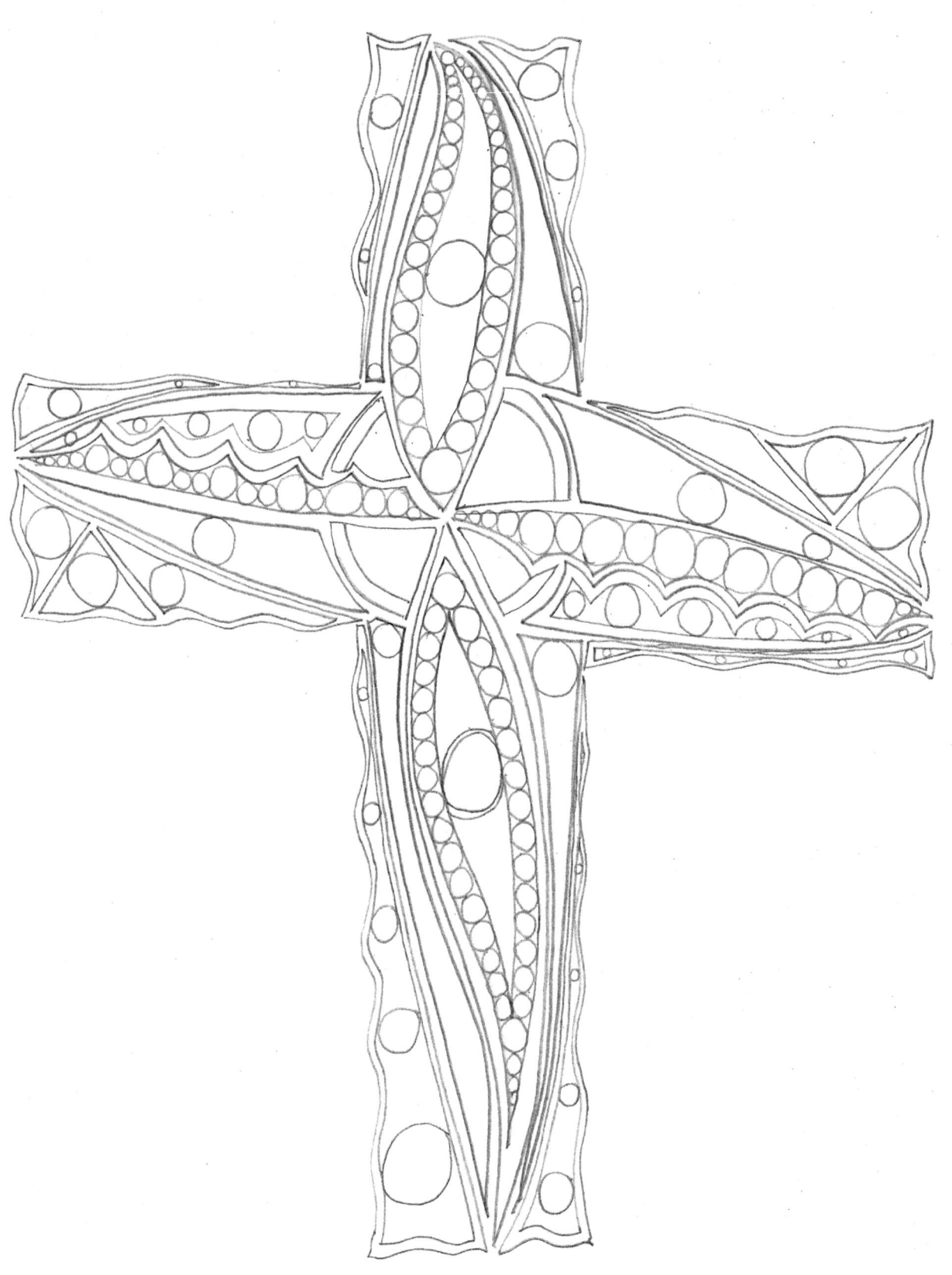

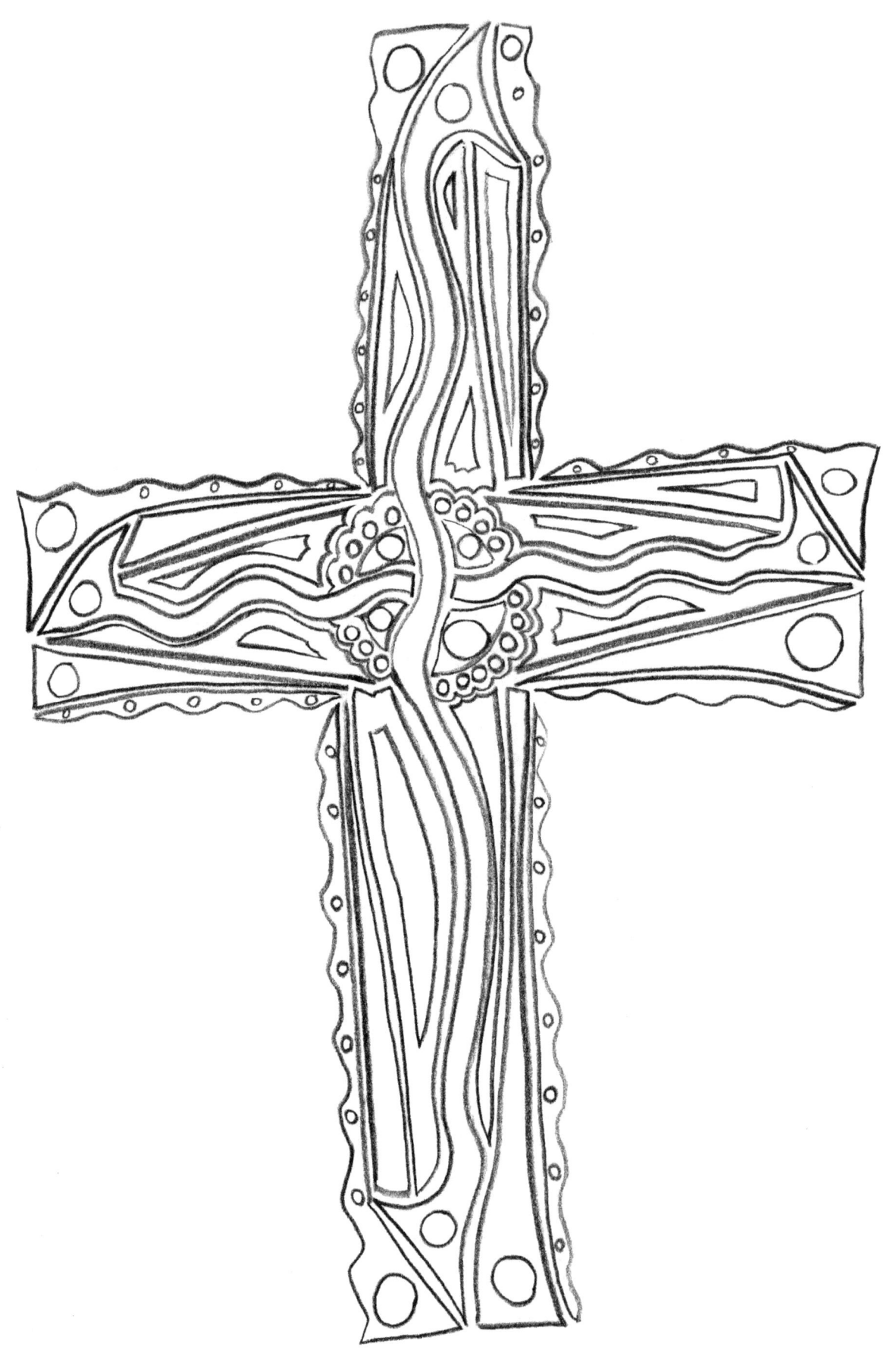

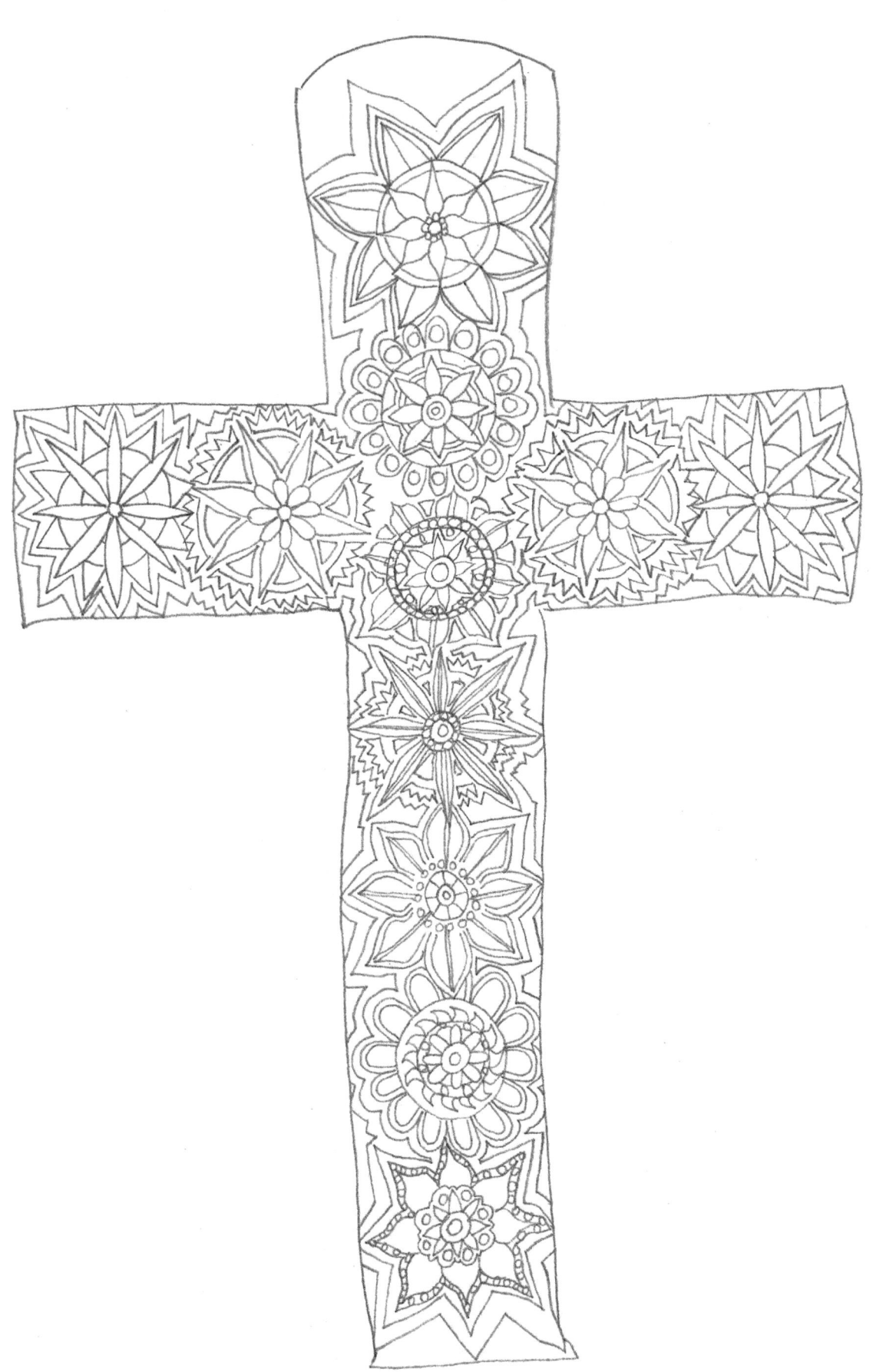

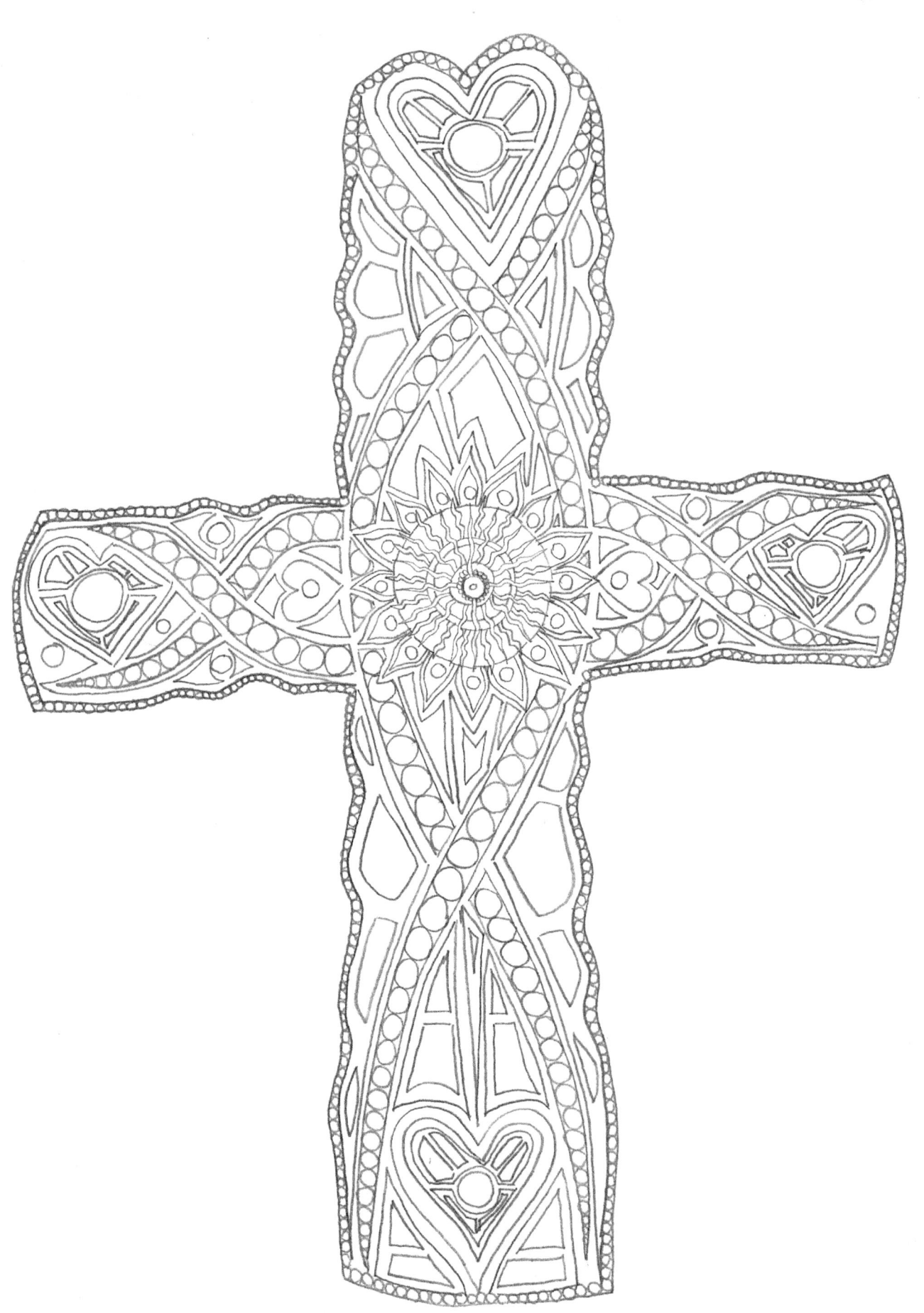

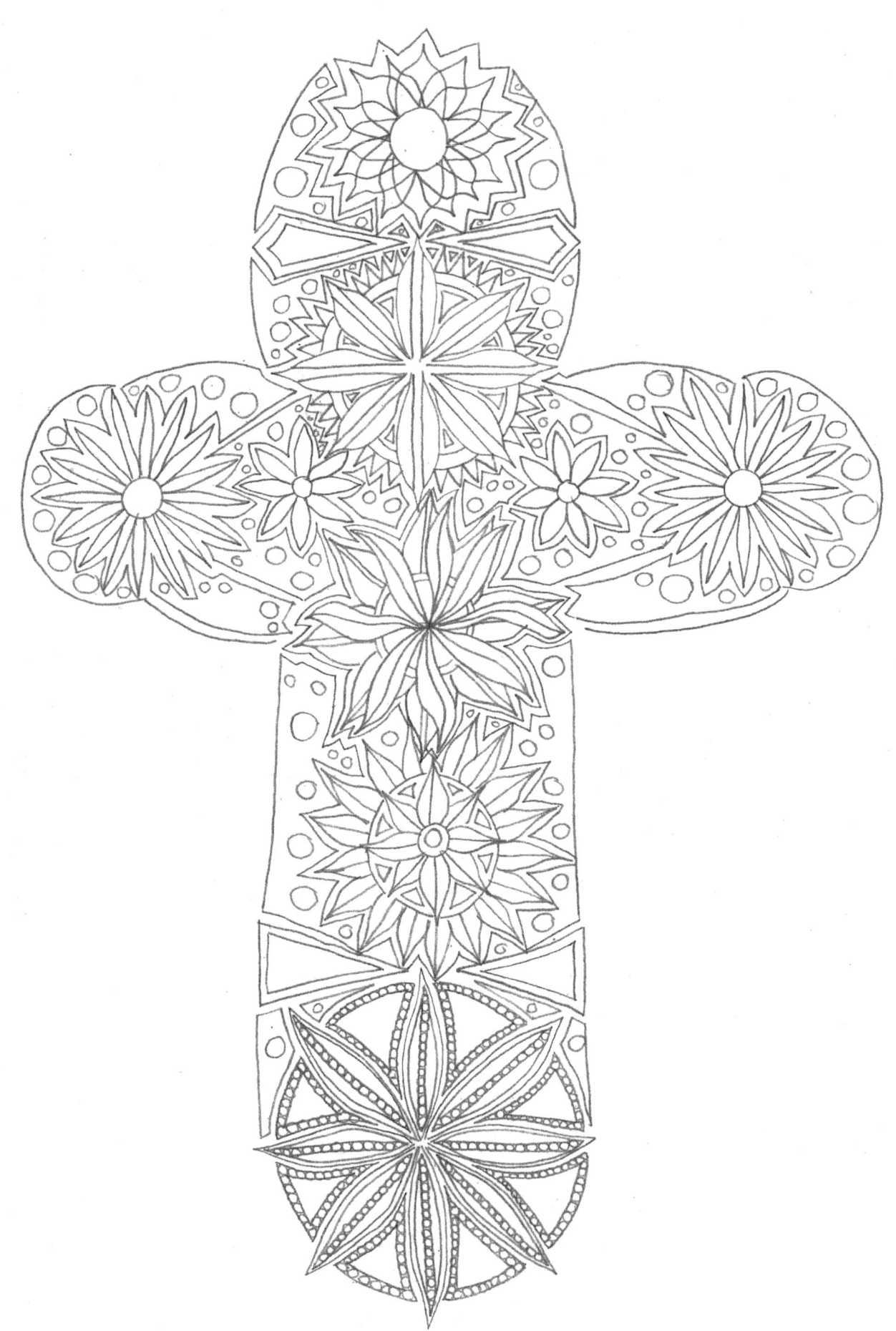

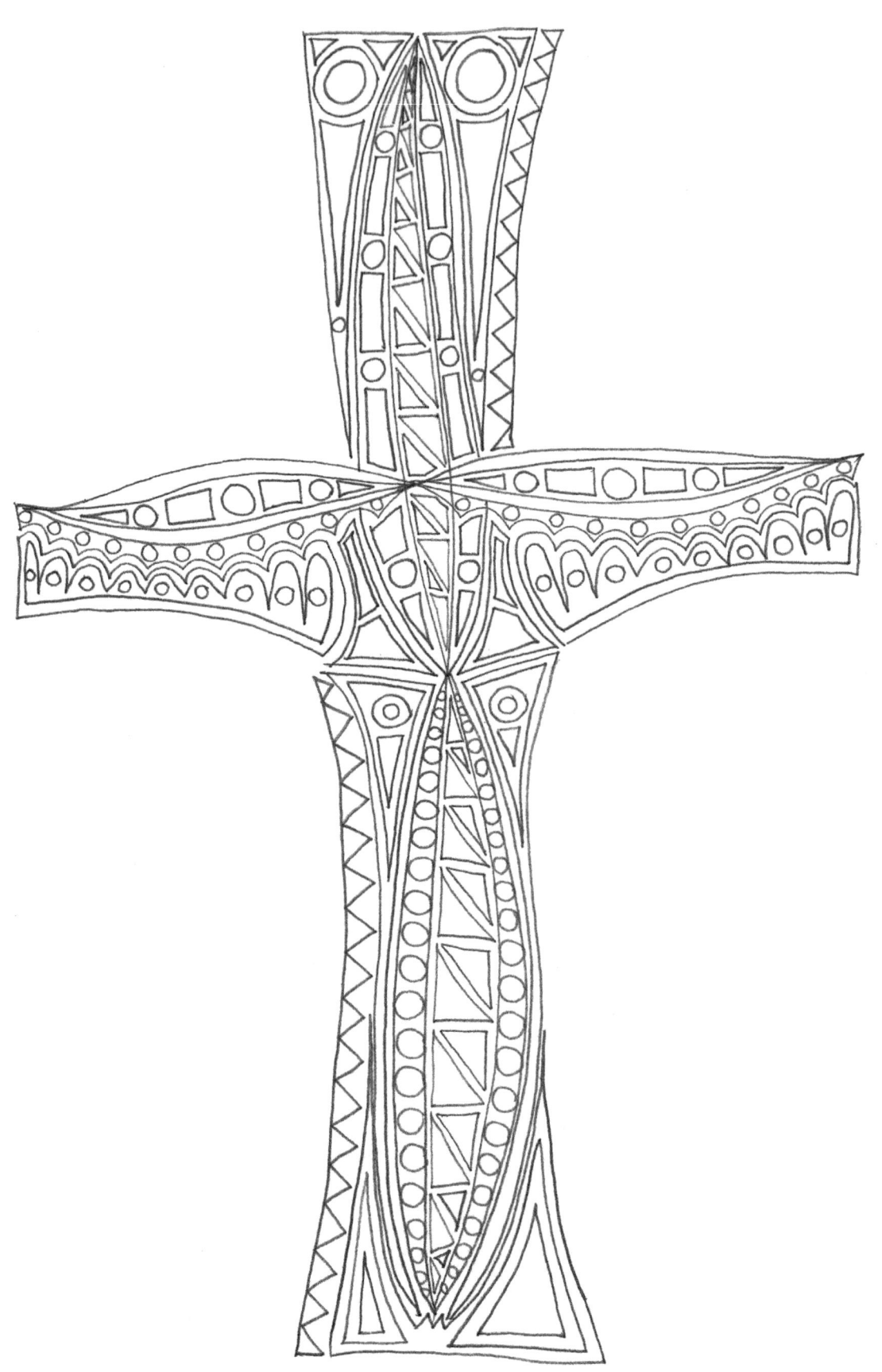

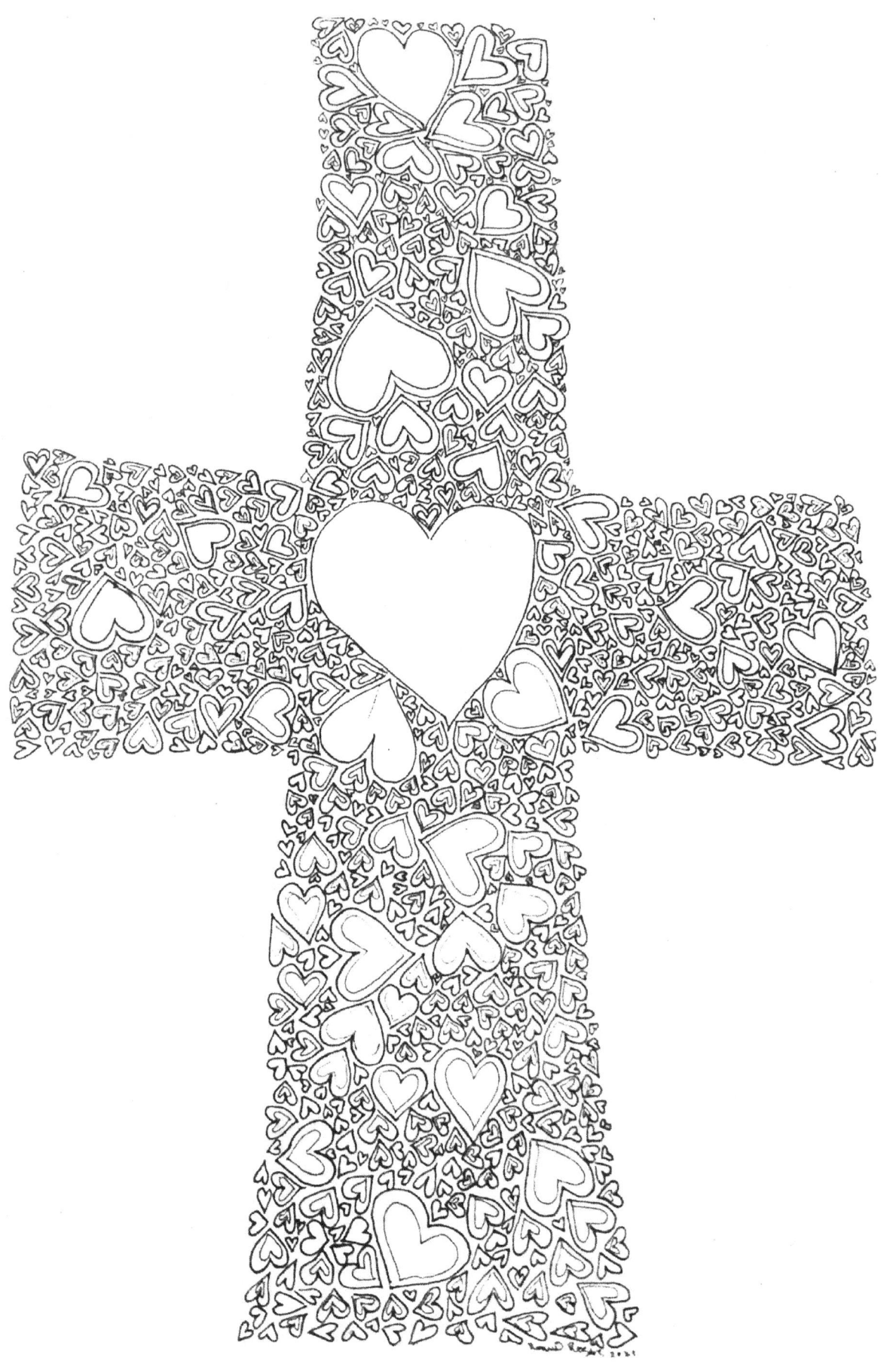

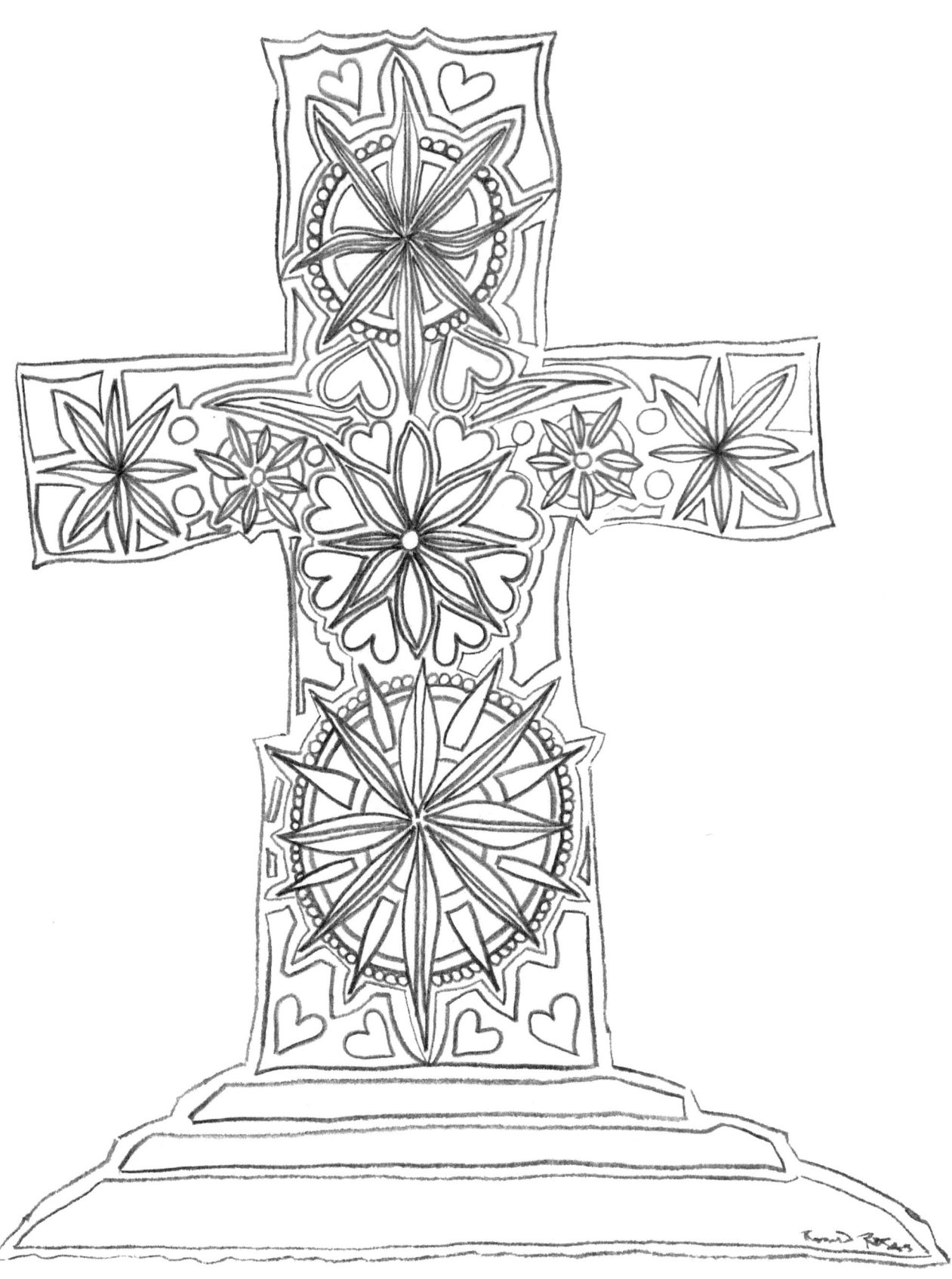

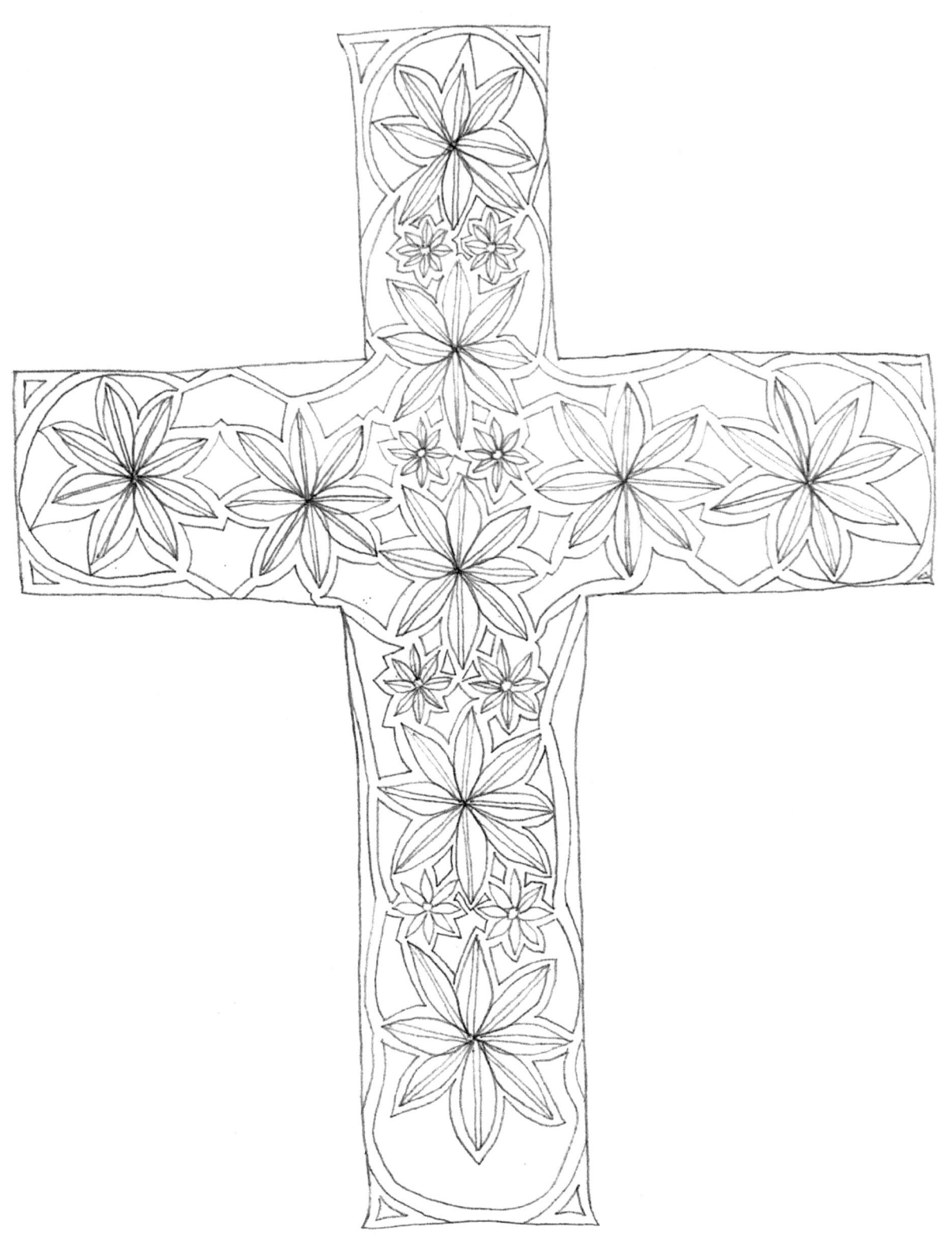

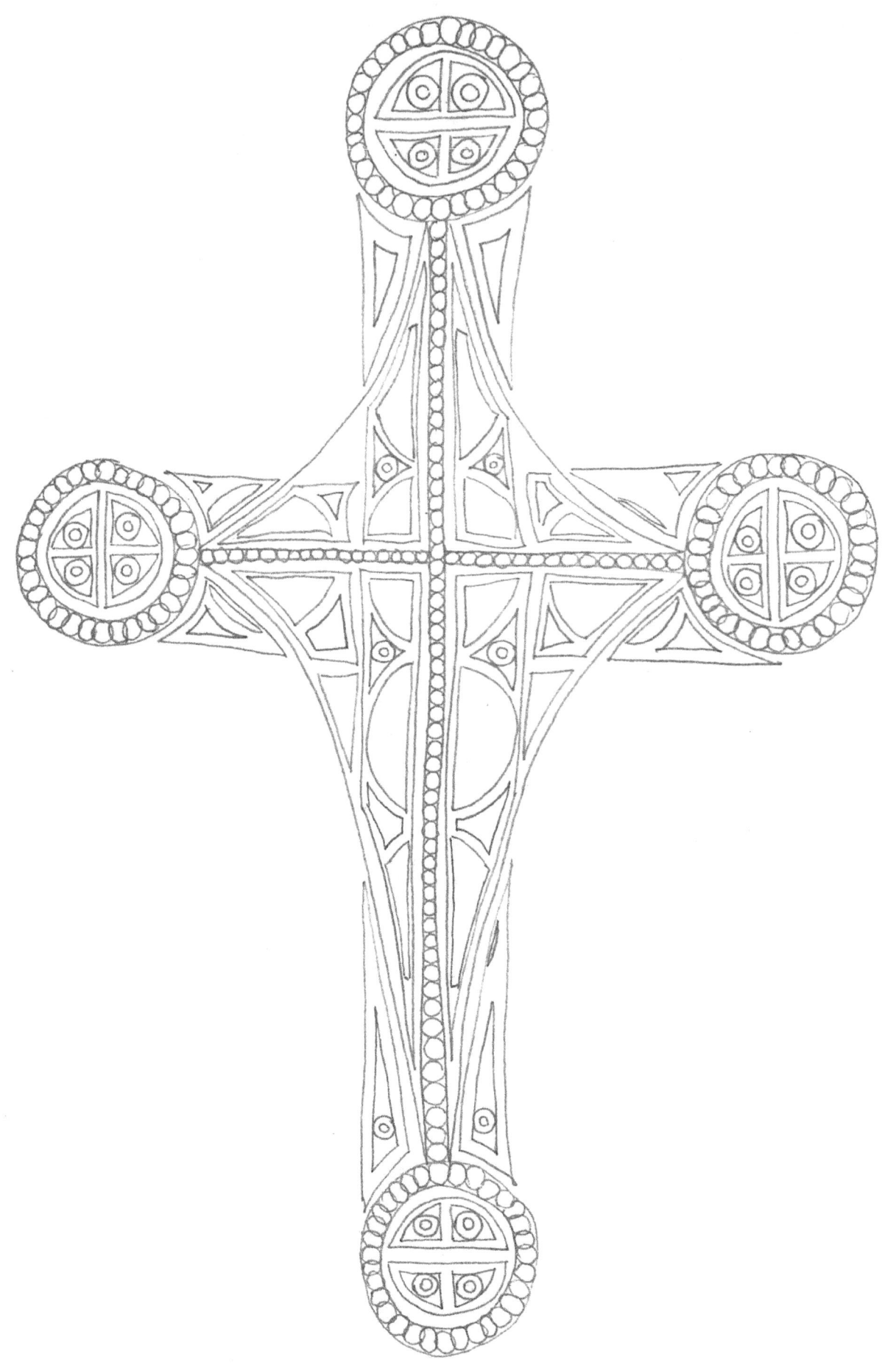

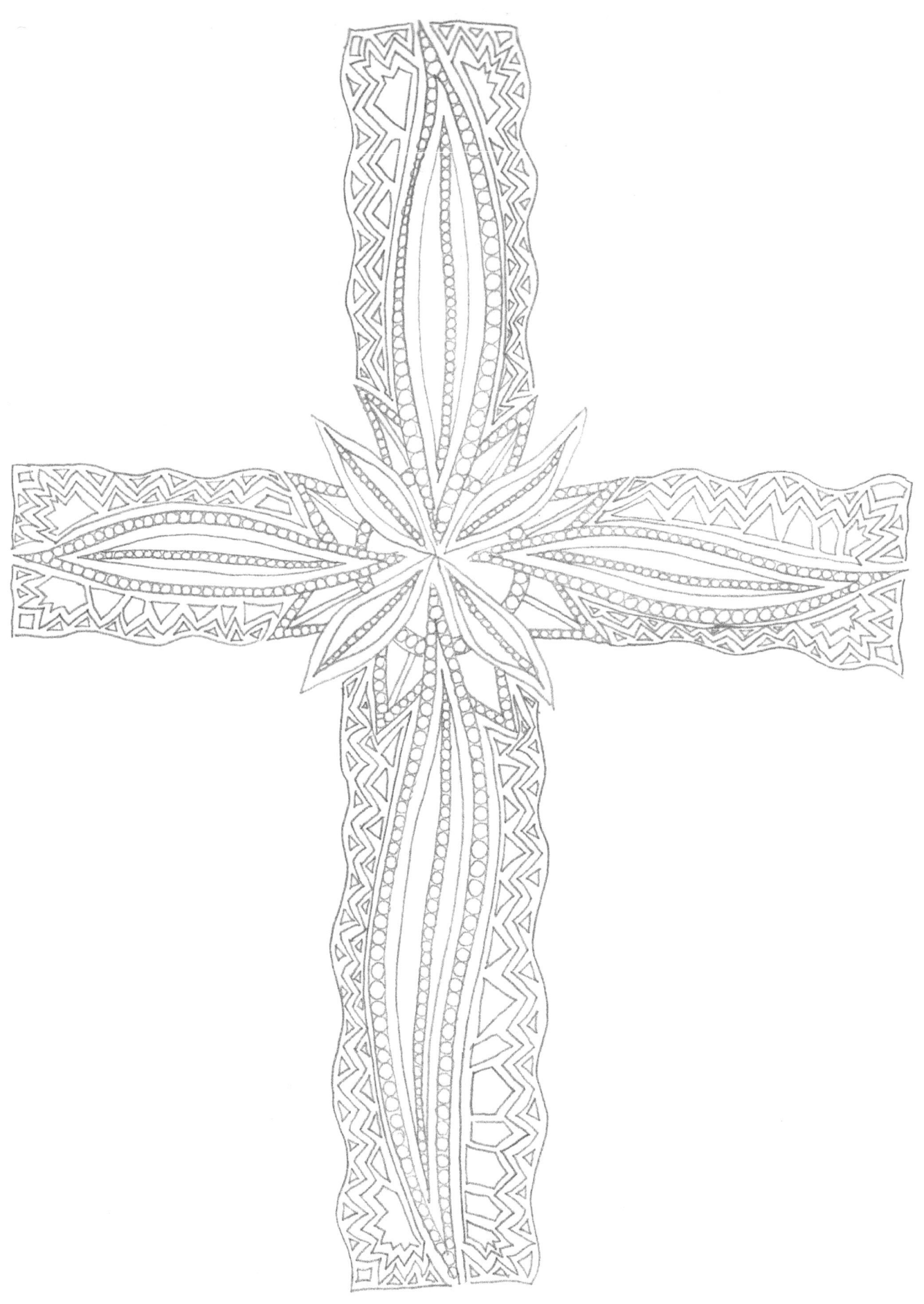

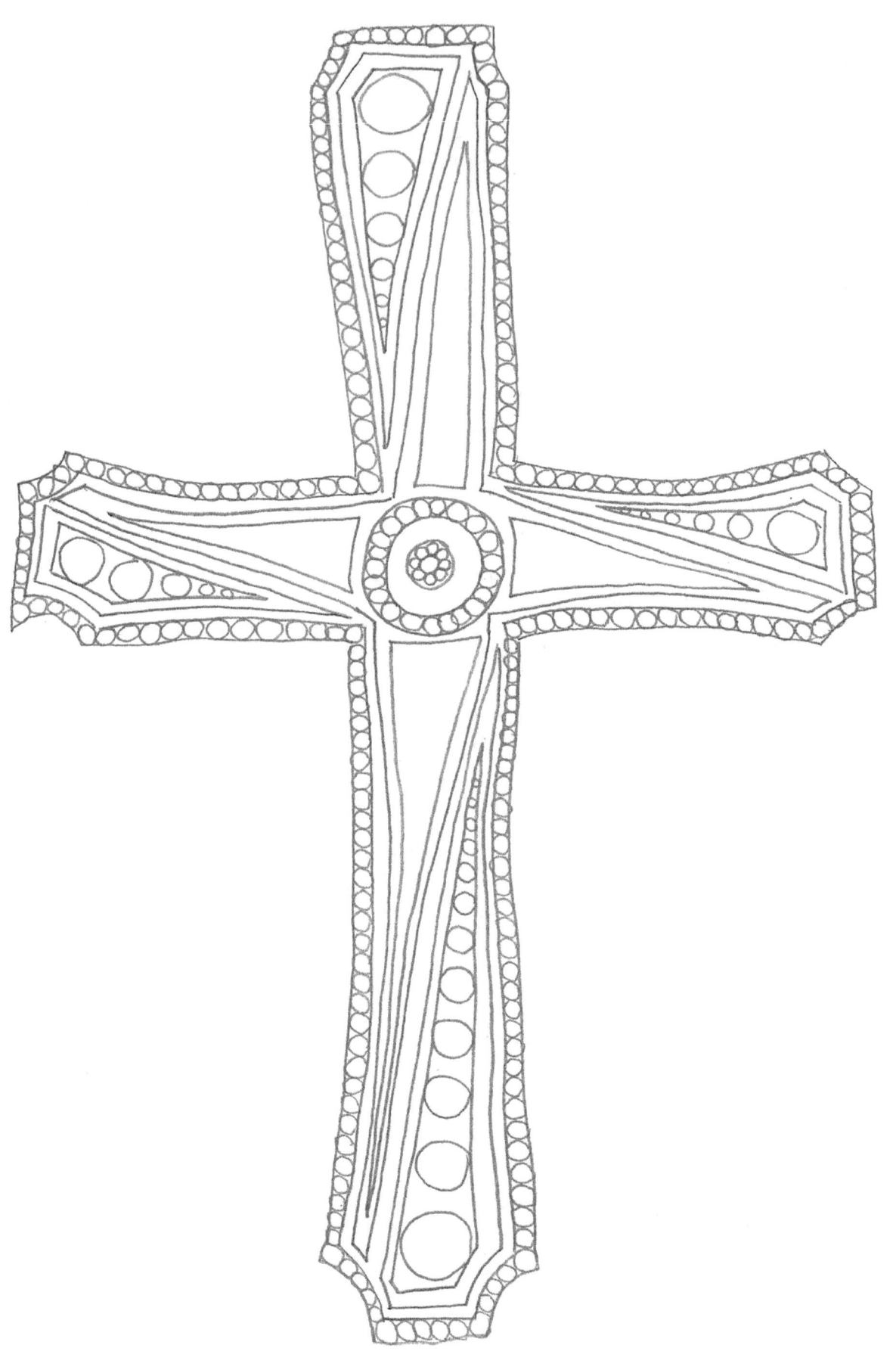

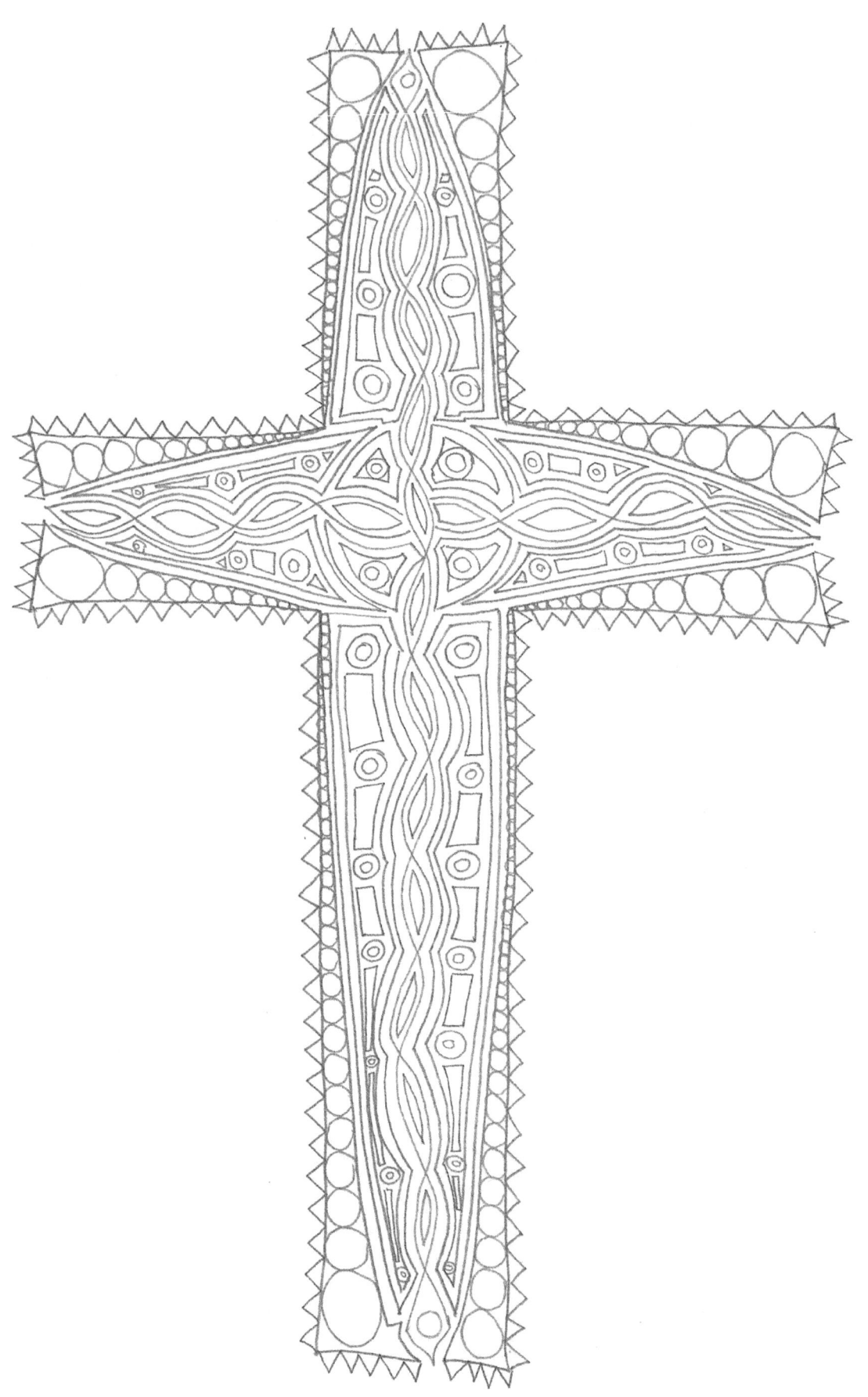

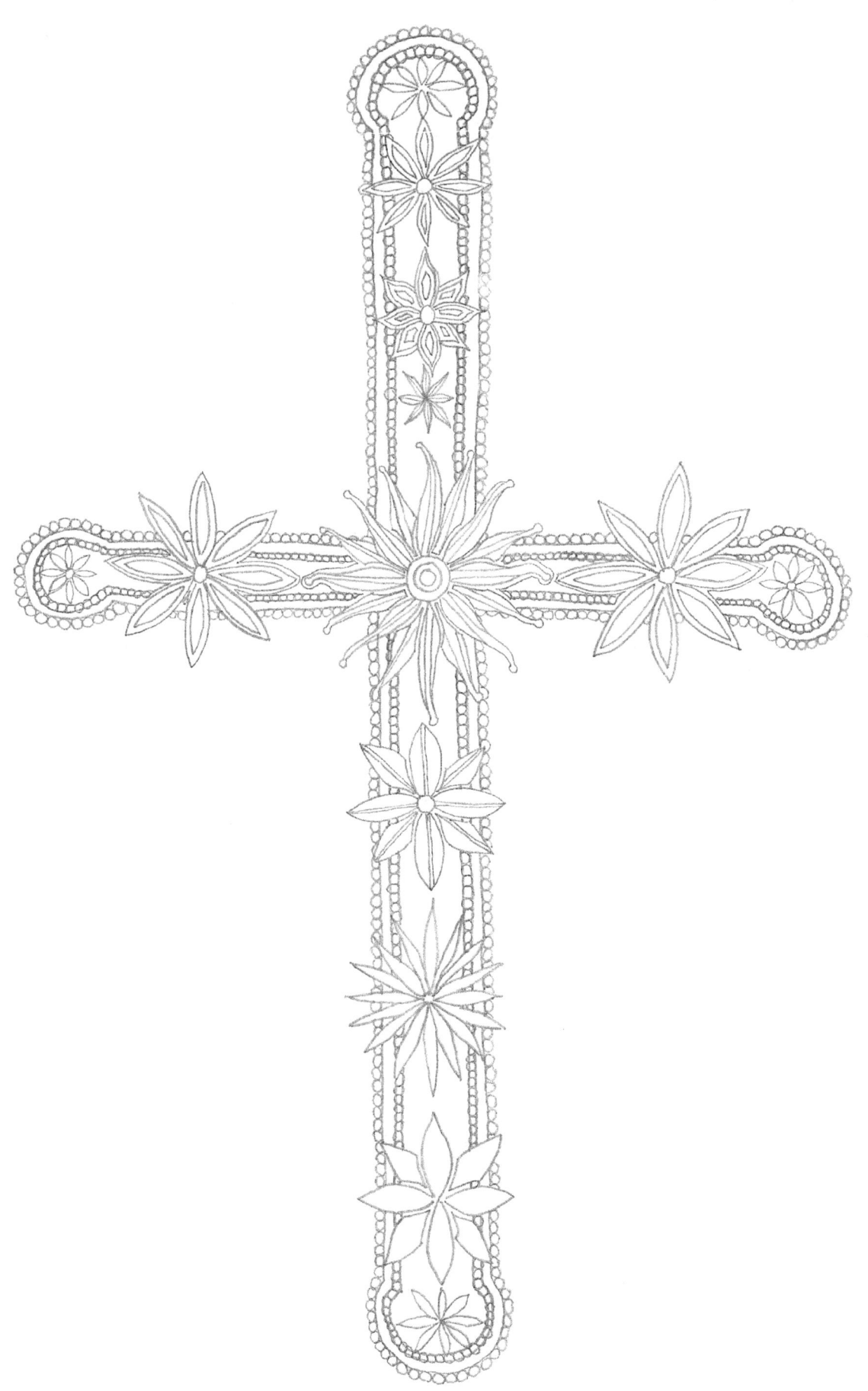

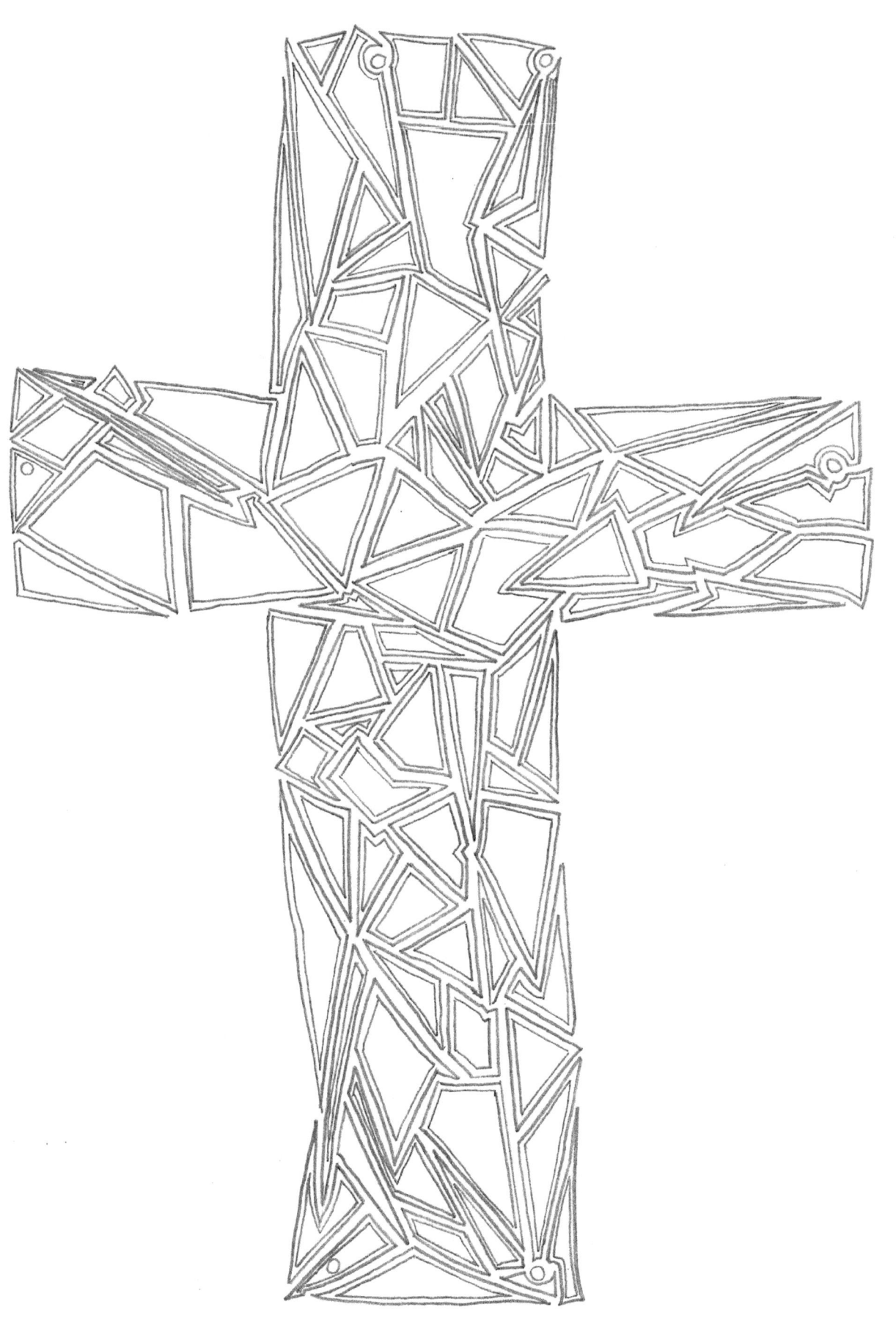

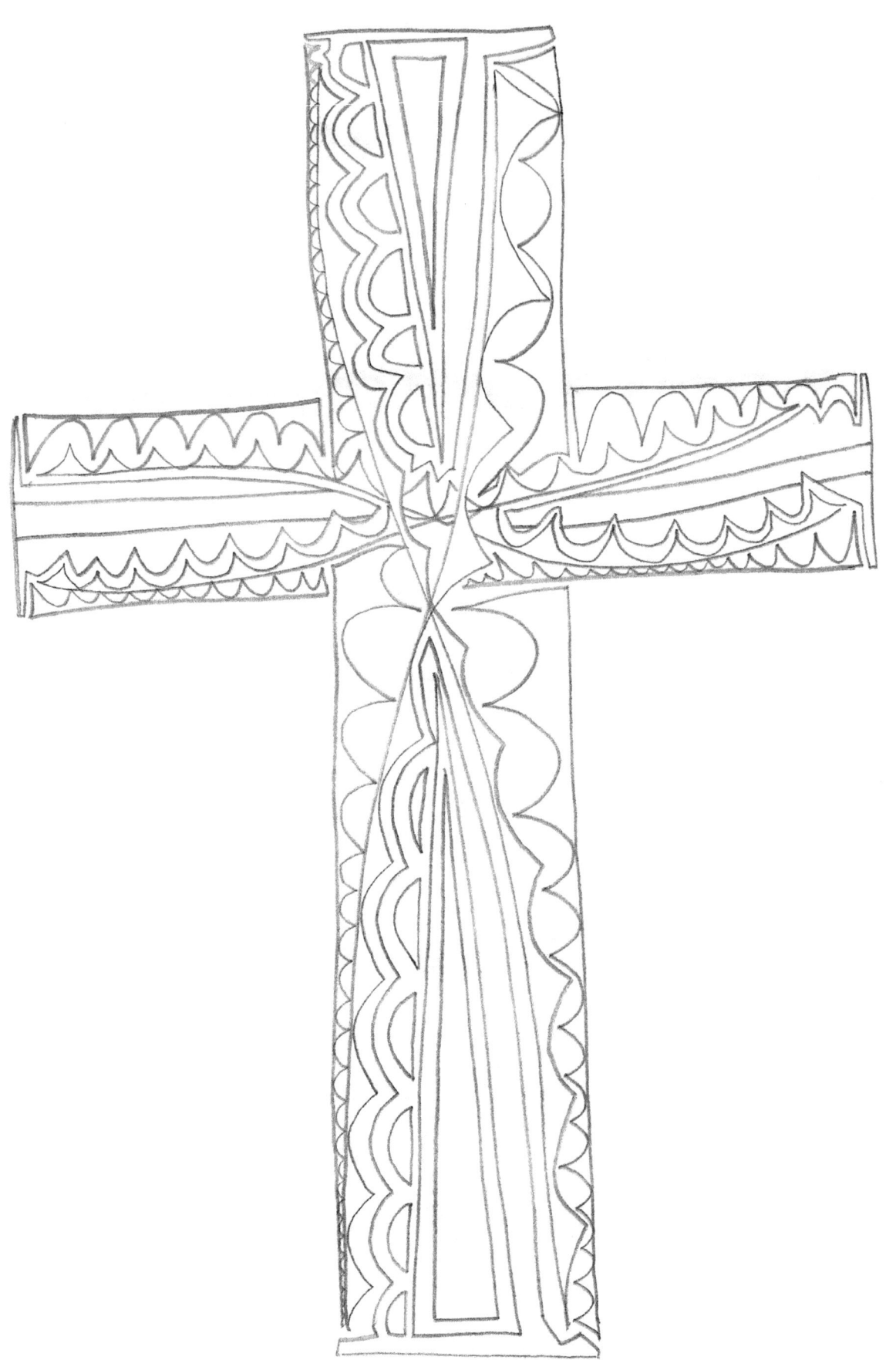

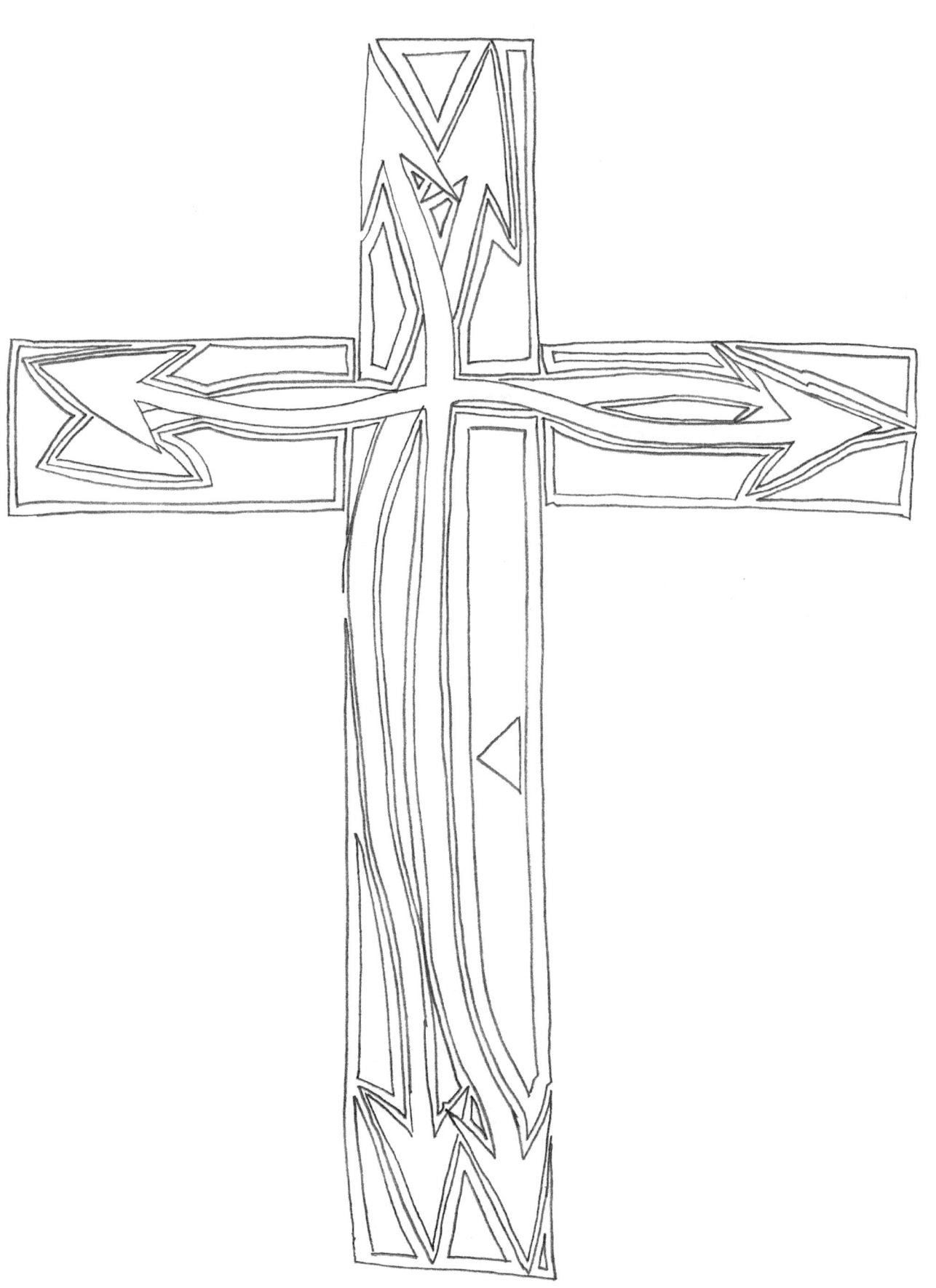

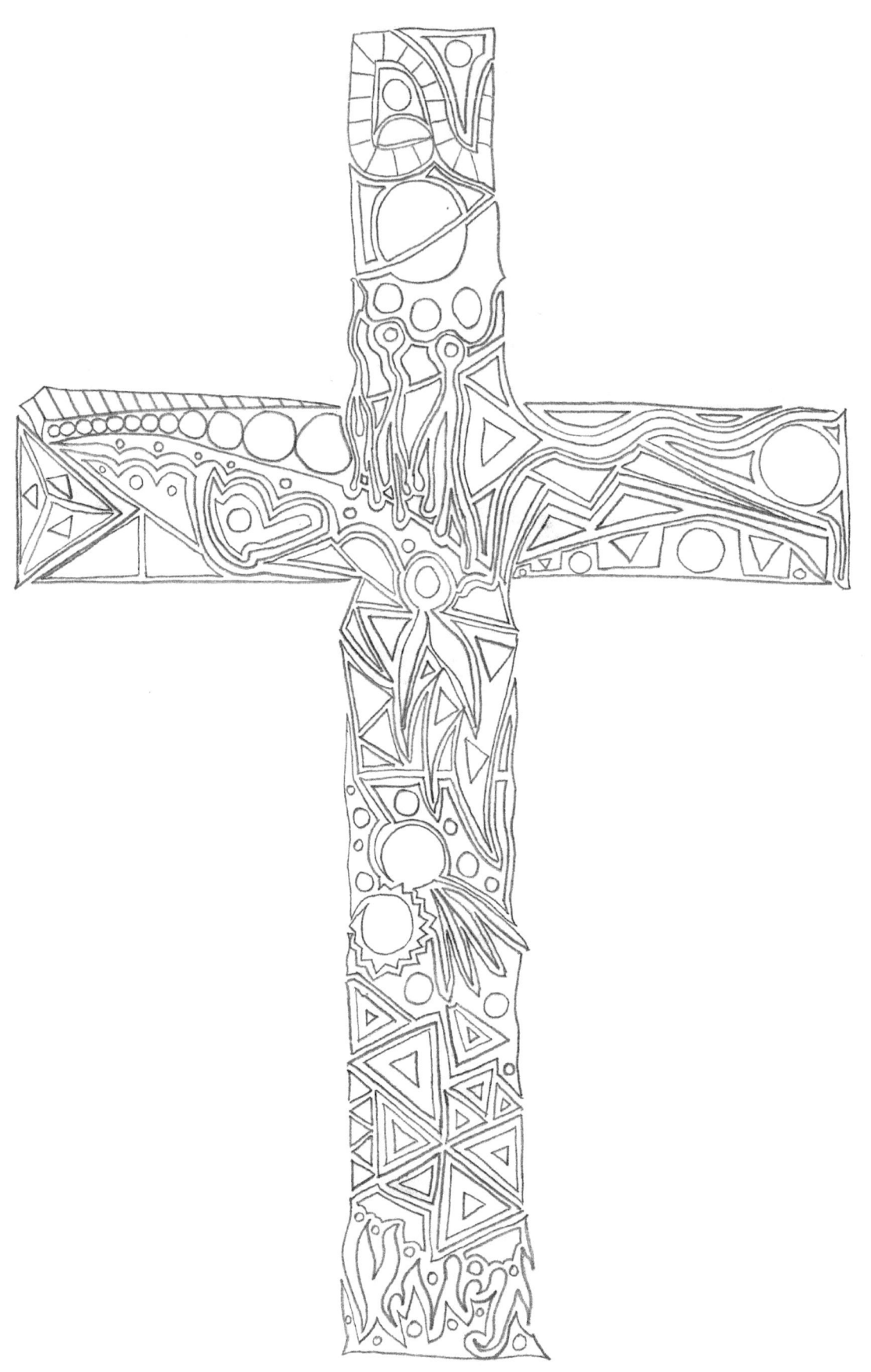

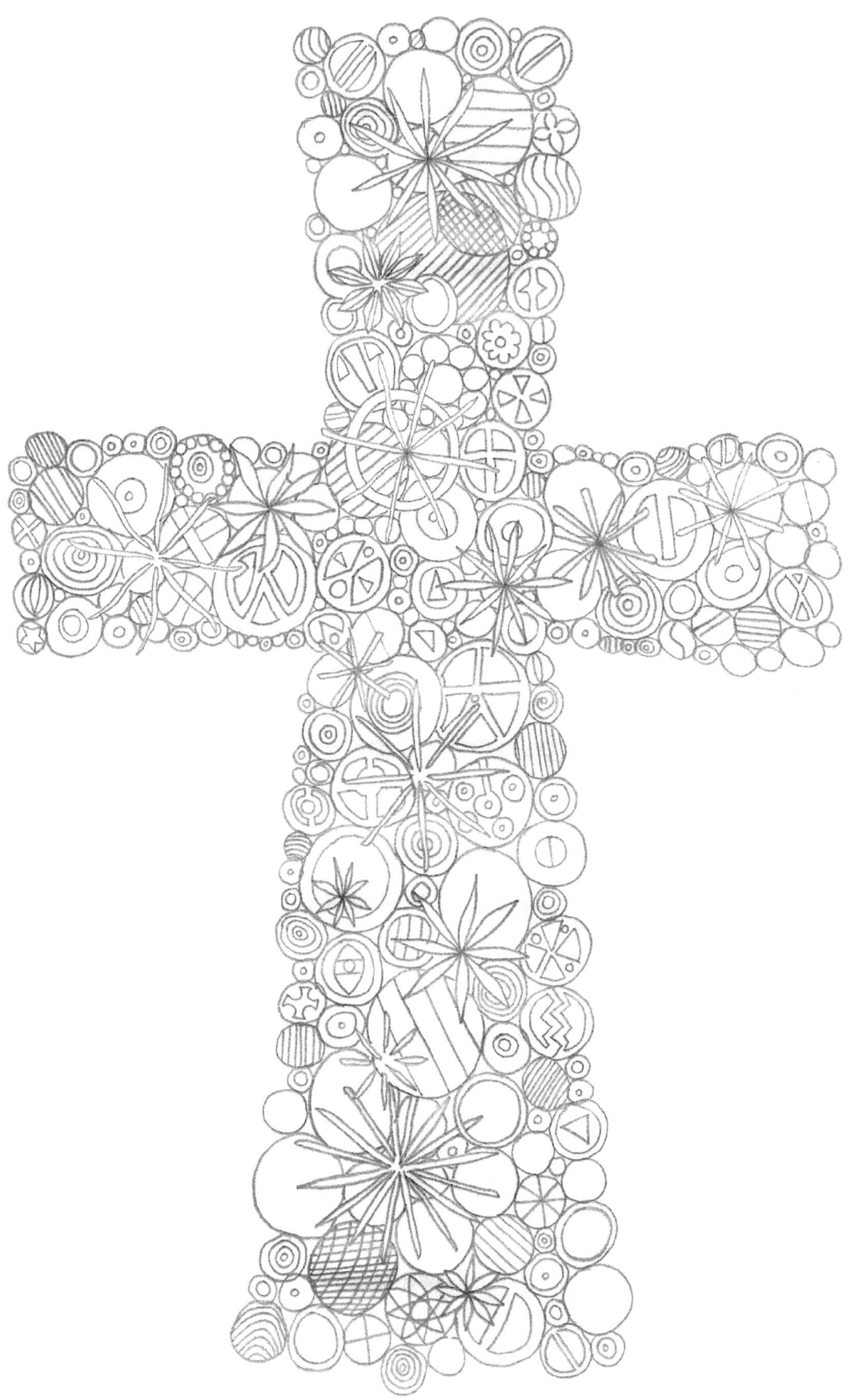

Cover Design by Art Duran
Illustrated by Ronnie Rosas
Edited by Art Duran

ISBN: SBN: 9798873908400
Imprint: Independently published
Kindle Direct Publishing
Printed in USA
Edition 2

ORDER

All Glory to God - Deuteronomy 32:2